# Secrets of the Sea

## The Story of Jeanne Power, Revolutionary Marine Scientist

by Evan Griffith    Illustrated by Joanie Stone

Clarion Books

Houghton Mifflin Harcourt

Boston   New York

Clarion Books
3 Park Avenue
New York, New York 10016

Clarion Books is an imprint of Houghton Mifflin Harcourt Publishing Company.

hmhbooks.com

The illustrations in this book were done digitally in Photoshop.
The text was set in Magellan.

Library of Congress Cataloging-in-Publication Data is available.
ISBN 978-0-358-24432-5

Manufactured in China
SCP 10 9 8 7 6 5 4 3 2 1
4500815070

For Rebecca and Robert —E.G.

For my grandma, who also fell in love with Sicily —J.S.

Jeanne curled her toes in the sand and gazed out across the deep blue Mediterranean Sea.

Gentle waves washed the shore.

A salty breeze *whooshed* like a whispered secret.

It was her first day in Sicily.

A large island off the coast of Italy, Sicily was nothing like the tiny village in France where Jeanne had grown up. It was also a big change from bustling Paris, where she had worked as a seamstress.

Jeanne could sew anything. She had once designed a wedding gown for an Italian princess!

But when she married a merchant and moved to Sicily, she decided
to leave dressmaking behind and try something new.
What would she do?
Who would she become?

Jeanne explored the island.

She saw wild olive trees and cypresses swaying in the breeze, falcons and eagles soaring overhead, hares scampering over grassy hills, and porcupines foraging among the bushes.

Sometimes, when she looked
out to sea, she caught a glimpse
of a breaching whale or a leaping
swordfish.

Sicily was buzzing with life.
It gave Jeanne a wild idea.

She would become a naturalist, a kind of scientist who studies animals and plants.

The year was 1818. Women weren't encouraged to be scientists, but Jeanne didn't let that stop her. She taught herself about natural history by reading books and talking to other scientists on the island.

Then she got to work. She walked all over Sicily with a journal in hand, jotting notes about every interesting animal and plant she found, and sketching many of them, too. She even brought new friends back to her house to observe up close, including two martens and a tortoise!

But Jeanne wasn't content to study only land animals.

Every day the sea breeze whispered in her ear and her eyes turned to the Mediterranean.

She wanted to learn about the animals that swam beneath the waves.

She wanted to uncover the secrets of the sea.

But how could Jeanne study animals that live where humans can't even breathe?

Other naturalists studied the preserved bodies of dead sea creatures, but Jeanne wanted to study sea creatures as they *lived*. She wanted to meet them face-to-face. She wanted to see how they moved through the water, how they interacted with one another, how they grew and changed over time.

She put her mind to work. Maybe a tank would do the trick, she thought. A large tank made of clear glass, filled with salt water so animals could swim inside. That way, she could study live sea creatures in her own home!

Jeanne didn't know where to find such a tank . . .

. . . so she made one herself.

It wasn't so different from creating a dress.
First there was an image in her head. Then she
turned the image into a design.

Finally, the design became a new object—
an aquarium. It was one of the world's first
aquariums built for scientific study.

And Jeanne didn't stop there. She also designed wooden cages that could be anchored in shallow water, allowing her to observe animals in their natural habitat.

She had her equipment. Now all she needed were sea creatures to study.

The fishermen waved to Jeanne when she hurried down to the port. She visited them every day in search of animals for her tanks and cages, and they saved interesting sea creatures for her in buckets of salt water.

The fishermen didn't see anything special about a bunch of weird-looking animals. But Jeanne did. She gazed eagerly into each bucket as though it were a treasure chest.

With her aquariums and a steady supply of animals from the port, Jeanne was finally ready to study marine life.

Jeanne studied many creatures, from seahorses to sea stars. But her favorite was the paper nautilus, a small octopus that lives inside a thin white shell.

Jeanne loved the rich colors of the paper nautilus. She loved the graceful way it sails through the water. With her aquariums, she was able to do something no one had ever done before: observe this enchanting octopus alive and up close. And this careful study gave her the chance to solve a mystery that had puzzled scientists for ages.

When scientists can't agree on something, they like to argue—and they had been arguing for a *long* time about whether the paper nautilus created its shell or stole it from another animal.

Jeanne knew that she could use her aquariums to settle this argument once and for all.

She placed paper nautilus eggs inside a tank. Now she just had to wait for them to hatch. She pressed her face against the aquarium glass and waited, day after day . . .

. . . until the baby octopuses emerged!

At first there were no signs of shells. Maybe paper
nautiluses steal their shells after all, Jeanne thought.
But to be sure, she kept watching.

Then, finally, she saw them: tiny shells, just
starting to take shape.

Jeanne's heart leaped. She had solved the mystery of the paper nautilus. It didn't steal another animal's shell—it created one of its own!

Jeanne spent several years studying sea creatures in Sicily, and she made many discoveries.

She witnessed the paper nautilus repairing cracks in its shell, which further proved that the shell was created, not stolen.

She observed octopuses holding stones with their tentacles and using them as tools.

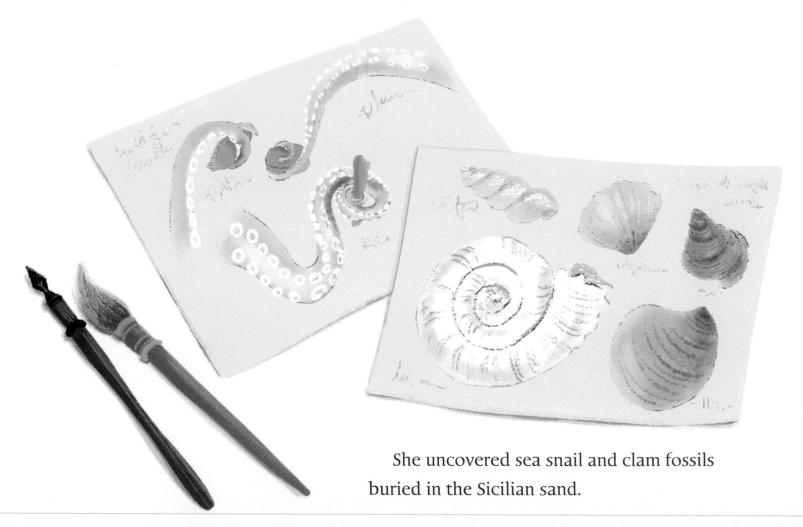

She uncovered sea snail and clam fossils buried in the Sicilian sand.

When she presented her findings at a nearby academy—a place where people gather to discuss science and share their research—her fellow scientists were impressed, and Jeanne became the academy's first female member.

Jeanne knew that her work was groundbreaking, and she wanted to present it to academies beyond Sicily, too. When she and her husband left Sicily to move to England, she had a wealth of research just waiting to be shared with the wider world.

But during the move, disaster struck.

Jeanne traveled by land, but she sent her belongings—including much of her research—by boat. Along the coast of France, the boat ran into a terrible storm . . .

. . . and sank.

When Jeanne heard the news, her heart sank, too. Most of her work was lost to the bottom of the sea, deep down where the octopuses dwell.

How would she share her discoveries with other scientists now?

Without her research, who would believe her?

Jeanne didn't give up. She returned to Sicily, rolled up
her sleeves, and went back to work.

She repeated her experiments.

She published her research so others could read it.

She shared her findings with a prestigious scientific academy in London.

At first, many people doubted Jeanne. They distrusted a female scientist, and they refused to believe that the paper nautilus created its shell.

But Jeanne's work was careful. Detailed. Precise. When she presented her evidence, it left no room for doubt.

Slowly, the world began to accept the truth of her discoveries.

It was never an easy road, but Jeanne stood her ground at every turn.
When a male scientist tried to take credit for solving the mystery of the
paper nautilus, Jeanne spoke out, reminding the scientific community that it
was her discovery.

Later, when the world began to forget Jeanne's contributions to aquarium design, she put pen to paper. "As I was the first to have the idea to study marine animals in aquariums and cages, I want to keep my rights as an inventor," she wrote in a letter to Richard Owen, an influential fellow scientist.

Jeanne joined many scientific academies throughout her life, a rare feat for a woman in the nineteenth century. Her research was published in several languages, and she earned the respect of her peers.

This respect wasn't just for her discovery that the paper nautilus creates
its shell. With her aquariums, Jeanne paved the way for the study of living sea
creatures. She brought humans and the sea closer together than ever before.

As Jeanne grew old, her thoughts never strayed far from the sea. Wherever she was, she could close her eyes and picture the deep blue of the Mediterranean. She could hear the gentle waves lapping the shore. She could smell the salt-tinged breeze.

She had unlocked some of the secrets of the sea, but she knew there were many more just waiting to be revealed by other curious minds. Others who looked out to sea and dared to wonder.

To explore.

To discover.

# Jeanne's Life and Legacy

*"I never thought of giving up my business. . . .
I armed myself with patience and courage."*
—Jeanne Villepreux-Power

Jeanne Villepreux-Power photographed by
André-Adolphe-Eugène Disdéri in 1861

*"Naturalists owe much to the wisdom and the spirit
of observation of this lady who was able to shed a
definitive light on an issue of natural history."*
—Carmelo Maravigna,
one of Jeanne's fellow scientists

Jeanne Villepreux-Power (pronounced Zhawn VEE-a-pro POE-wear) was born on September 25, 1794, in the little village of Juillac in France. Although she did not receive a formal education as a child, she did learn how to read and write—most likely taught by her mother.

In 1812, when she was eighteen years old, Jeanne left home and moved to Paris to become a seamstress. There, she made a name for herself by designing the wedding gown for the Italian princess Marie-Caroline. Legend holds that Jeanne met her future husband, James Power, at the royal wedding.

Jeanne and James married in 1818, when Jeanne was twenty-three years old. They settled in Messina, a coastal city in the northeast corner of Sicily. Jeanne no longer had to make dresses for a living. Instead, she turned her mind to science and natural history. She traveled across the whole island, cataloging its plants, animals, towns, and natural wonders along the way. Later in life she used all this information to write and publish a highly praised travel guide to Sicily.

Jeanne is best known, though, for solving the mystery of the paper nautilus, as well as for her innovative aquariums, which she began building in 1832. There were three distinct designs: a glass tank that Jeanne kept in her house in Messina, which most resembles modern fish tanks; another tank covered in a wooden or iron cage that could be submerged in the sea and then extracted

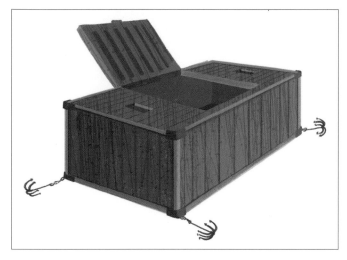
One of Jeanne's cages designed to be anchored in the sea

when Jeanne wanted to make observations; and a larger wooden cage that could be anchored in the shallow seabed. By using her sea aquariums to study marine animals in their natural environment, Jeanne worked much like a modern-day field zoologist.

Although aquariums have existed in various forms since ancient times, Jeanne was one of the first to create aquariums specifically for scientific observation. This put her at the forefront of a major shift in how animals were studied. In the nineteenth century, scientists were moving away from the practice of studying and classifying dead animals, and they were growing increasingly curious about animal behavior—which meant, of course, that they had to study live specimens! By pioneering methods for observing living marine animals and writing about her procedures so other scientists could try them, too, Jeanne played a crucial role in this scientific revolution.

The way she advocated for her work was equally revolutionary. Jeanne was far from the only woman making game-changing scientific discoveries in the nineteenth century. Unfortunately, many female scientists of this era did not receive credit for their work. By speaking out when others tried to lay claim to her research, and by ensuring that her name was attached to her publications, she helped open the door for the recognition of women in science.

While Jeanne encountered resistance from many members of the scientific community, she also earned several honors during her lifetime. Her writings were published in Italian, French, English, and German, and she was welcomed as a member of several scientific academies throughout Europe, including the Zoological Society of London, a prestigious organization that counted Charles Darwin among its Fellows. She even inspired the name of a species of lightfish: *Vinciguerria poweriae.*

Jeanne died in 1871 in her hometown of Juillac. Much later, in 1997, a huge crater on Venus was named in her honor, celebrating her remarkable achievements. Jeanne may have studied the seas, but she found her place among the stars.

# The Paper Nautilus

Although Jeanne studied many sea creatures during her time in Sicily, her heart belonged to the paper nautilus, also called *Argonauta*. She thought the creature was beautiful, writing, "When the air is calm, the sea calm, and it thinks itself unobserved, it is then that the *Argonauta* is adorned with its beauties." But she also found it to be quite mischievous—she recounts paper nautiluses splashing her with water and snatching food right out of her hands!

Jeanne's watercolor painting of a paper nautilus

Like other octopuses, paper nautiluses have eight arms. They are relatively small, with females growing up to a foot long and males measuring at under an inch (all the paper nautiluses that Jeanne observed were female; the tiny male paper nautiluses were not officially discovered until after her studies). They live in tropical and subtropical waters, feeding on jellyfish, crustaceans, and mollusks. When under attack by a predator, they release ink, which clouds the water and gives them a chance to escape.

A paper nautilus tucked into its shell

The pale white "shell" of the female paper nautilus is actually an egg case. As Jeanne discovered, the creature secretes the shell from its two front arms. In addition to carrying eggs (up to a whopping 170,000 at a time), the shell can hold air, allowing the paper nautilus to maintain buoyancy in the ocean.

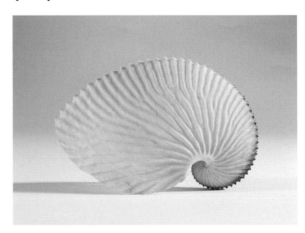
A paper nautilus shell

No two shells are exactly alike—each one is as individual as the paper nautilus that creates it. Sometimes the shells wash up on the shore, so the next time you visit the beach, keep an eye out!

# Marine Biology and Conservation

Jeanne's legacy lives on through the evolving work of marine biology. Amazing technologies such as sonar mapping, underwater vehicles, and ocean-exploring robots have given us access to the seas in ways that scientists in Jeanne's day could only dream about. Still, there's a lot we don't know yet. Although water covers almost three-quarters of our planet's surface, much of the ocean remains unexplored by humans. And new deep-sea creatures are being discovered all the time!

For many scientists, studying the sea inspires a desire to protect it and its amazing resources. As Jeanne was working in Sicily, she realized that some bodies of water were overfished. Overfishing occurs when people catch too many fish and there aren't enough animals left in the water. Jeanne came up with a solution: raising fish in underwater cages, much like the cages that she designed for study, and then releasing the fish in the overfished water to repopulate it.

Today, the world's oceans face a number of challenges, from pollution to climate change. But like Jeanne, we can all find a way to help. If you live near a beach, you might organize a beach cleanup day with your friends or classmates. Wherever you live, though, small steps—like using fewer plastic products and recycling whenever possible—can make a big difference.

To find out more about how scientists are taking action to protect the wonders of the sea, you can look into these marine conservation organizations:

Oceana (oceana.org)

The Marine Conservation Institute (marine-conservation.org)

Ocean Conservancy (oceanconservancy.org)

# Note on Historical Research

Researching historical events can present challenges. Sometimes there aren't enough sources to know exactly what happened or exactly when it happened. Other times, sources don't agree with each other. For example, some accounts of Jeanne's story say that the shipwreck in which she lost much of her work occurred in 1843, the year that she left Sicily for good and ended her studies of sea creatures.

However, by digging deeper and talking to experts on Jeanne's life, I found strong evidence that the shipwreck actually took place several years earlier, during Jeanne's first move to England. Several sources, including shipping records, date the ship's ill-fated journey to 1838, and this timeline is supported by Jeanne herself: In an article she published in 1842 in a Sicilian scientific journal, Jeanne mentioned the loss of her earlier work in a shipwreck while reporting on the new studies of the paper nautilus that she had been conducting since returning to Sicily. That's why this book places the shipwreck in 1838.

When you find contradictions in research, the best thing you can do is dig as deeply as you can, look for the strongest evidence, and be honest about the questions you faced and how you sought to answer them.

# Bibliography

### Primary Sources

Power, Giovanna [Villepreux-Power, Jeanne]. *Guida per la Sicilia*. Naples: Stabilimento Poligrafico di Filippo Cirelli, 1842. [Reprint ed. by M. D'Angelo, Messina 1995 and Messina 2008.]

Villepreux-Power, Jeanne. Letter to Professor Richard Owen. Aug. 21, 1857.

Villepreux-Power, Jeanne. *Observations physiques sur le poulpe de l'Argonauta argo: commencées en 1832 et terminées en 1843, dédiées À M. Le Professeur Owen F.R.S.* 1856.

Villepreux-Power, Jeanne. *Observations et expériences physiques sur la Bulla lignaria, l'Astérias, l'Octopus vulgaris et la Pina nobilis.* 1860.

Maravigna, Carmelo. "Compte-rendu des observations et expériences de Madame Power sur l'Argonaute Argo." Messina, Stamperia Fiumara, 1836.

### Secondary Sources

Allcock, et al. "The Role of Female Cephalopod Researchers: Past and Present." *Journal of Natural History,* vol. 49, no. 21-24, 2015, pp. 1235–66, doi:10.1080/00222933.2015.1037088.

Arnal, Claude. "Jeanne Villepreux-Power, A Pioneering Environmental Malacologist." Malacological Society of London - Bulletin Board, www.malacsoc.org.uk/malacological_bulletin/BULL34/JEANNE.htm.

D'Angelo, Michela. "Da Cenerentola a Dama Degli Argonauti: Jeannette Villepreux Power a Messina (1818–1843)." *Naturalista Sicil,* S. IV, XXXVI (2), 2012, pp. 191–224.

Fessenden, Marissa. "A 19th Century Shipwreck Might Be Why This Famous Female Naturalist Faded to Obscurity." Smithsonian.com, Smithsonian Institution, June 2, 2015, www.smithsonianmag.com/smart-news/19th-century-shipwreck-might-be-why-famous-female-naturalists-name-faded-obscurity-180955468/.

Parsons, Eleanor. "The Lady and the Argonauts." *New Scientist,* vol. 233, no. 3114, 2017, pp. 40–41. doi:10.1016/S0262-4079(17)30374-3.

Scales, Helen. *Spirals in Time: The Secret Life and Curious Afterlife of Seashells.* Bloomsbury Sigma, 2015.

Young, Lauren J. "The Seamstress and the Secrets of the Argonaut Shell." *Science Friday,* June 20, 2018, www.sciencefriday.com/articles/the-seamstress-and-the-secrets-of-the-argonaut-shell/.

The author would like to extend special thanks to the scientists, journalists, and historians who shared insights and research, including Michela D'Angelo, Josquin Debaz, Lauren J. Young, Jennifer Coston-Guarini, and Louise Allcock.